Easy Homemade Christmas Gifts 2014:

DIY Gifts For Everyone You Know!

By: Katie Cotton

Easy Homemade Christmas Gifts 2014

TABLE OF CONTENTS

TABLE OF CONTENTS 2

PUBLISHERS NOTES 7

DEDICATION 8

CHAPTER 1- 9 EASY TO MAKE CHRISTMAS GIFT IDEAS FOR KIDS 9

SOFTEST PLAY DOUGH 9

DRAWING JOURNAL 10

GREAT KEEPSAKE 11

POPSICLE STICK PUZZLES 11

MELTING GIANT WAX CRAYONS 12

CHRISTMAS SWEATER BABY LEG WARMERS 12

DIY DRUMS FOR YOUR LITTLE DRUMMER BOY 13

COLORFUL JUGGLING BALLS 14

TOY SOAP 14

CHAPTER 2- AWESOME DIY CHRISTMAS GIFT IDEAS FOR FRIENDS 16

LOTION, NAIL FILE GIFT BOX 16

HOMEMADE BEESWAX CANDLES 17

DIY STUDDED PHONE CASE 18

BEACH PHOTO JAR 19

DIY PHOTO COASTERS.. 20

CRANBERRY LIME VODKA 21

LET IT SNOW TREAT JARS 21

CUPCAKE IN A JAR 22

CHAPTER 3- BEST HANDMADE GIFTS FOR MEN 24

INTERCHANGEABLE LEGO STAR WARS CLOCK 24

MONOGRAM MUGS.. 25

KEYBOARD MESSAGE.. 27

JACK DANIEL'S SOAP DISPENSER 27

PHOTO BOOKMARK 28

UPCYCLED HANDLEBAR BAG 28

LAPTOP DESK WITH A CHALKBOARD TO TAKE NOTES........ 29

HAND PRINTED MOUSE PAD 30

CHAPTER 4- FUN TO MAKE CHRISTMAS GIFTS IDEAS FOR GIRL FRIENDS.. 32

PERSONALIZED CANDLE 33

SPA IN A JAR 34

OATMEAL BATH BOMBS 34

POT HOLDER PURSE CADDY 35

DIY PHOTO GIFT 35

RIC RAC ROSE 36

TEACUP CANDLES 37

CHAPTER 5- UNDER 5 DOLLARS DIY CHRISTMAS GIFT IDEAS 38

HOMEMADE LEMON SOAP 38

IPAD KITCHEN TABLET HOLDER 39

JAR LID PICTURE MAGNETS 39

SNOW GLOBE NECKLACE 40

LEAF-IMPRINTED CLAY NECKLACE 41

SHOWER CURTAIN RING BRACELETS 42

ADJUSTABLE RIBBON BRACELET 43

YARN WRAPPED CANDLES 44

CHAPTER 6- 15 CUTE HOMEMADE GIFTS, KIDS CAN MAKE 45

HANDPRINT SNOWMAN ORNAMENT 45

SNOW GLOBE JAR 46

PICTURESQUE CORKBOARDS 46

POLKA DOT FLOWER VASE 46

DIY PAPERWEIGHT 47

PINWHEEL NECKLACE 47

WOODEN BEADED NECKLACE 47

HANDPRINT TREE APRON 48

CUSTOMIZED TRAY 48

HANDY COASTERS 48

BEAUTIFUL BOTTLE PRINTS 48

PICTURE FRAME ORNAMENT 49

VOTIVE CANDLE HOLDERS 49

EMBROIDERED FELT PURSE 49

FABRIC NECKLACE 50

CHAPTER 7- 5 LOVELY GIFTS YOU CAN MAKE FOR YOUR GRANNIES 51

A CHRISTMAS GIFT FOR GRANDMA 52

GRANDMA BLOCKS! 52

MOD PODGED ORNAMENTS 53

COUNT YOUR BLESSINGS BOARD 54

HANDPRINT TREES WRAPPED CANVAS 55

CHAPTER 8- 10 TOTALLY DO-ABLE DIY CHRISTMAS GIFT IDEAS USING MASON JARS. 57

CHRISTMAS CANDIES GIFT JAR 57

MASON JAR CANDY PEDESTALS 58

PERSONALIZED MASON JAR DRINK 59

DIY LAVENDER BATH SALTS 60

DIY PEPPERMINT SUGAR SCRUB 60

DIY LUXURIOUS HOMEMADE WHIPPED BODY BUTTER 60

SNOWY MASON JAR 61

MASON JAR SNOW GLOBE 61

A GORGEOUS MASON JAR CANDLE 62

MASON JAR SOAP DISPENSER 63

CHAPTER 9- HOMEMADE DOG-I-Y TREAT RECIPES 64

PEANUT BUTTER DOGGIE TREATS 64

PUMPKIN DOG BISCUITS 65

BACON DOG BISCUITS 66

SWEET POTATO DOG CHEW TREATS 66

HOMEMADE FLAX SEED DOG BISCUITS 67

EASY TWO-INGREDIENT HOMEMADE DOG TREATS 68

HOMEMADE DOG TREATS RECIPE 69

PAW-PRINT DOG TREATS 69

ABOUT THE AUTHOR 71

EXCERPT SECTION 72

Katie Cotton

PUBLISHERS NOTES

Disclaimer

The author and publisher specifically disclaim all responsibility for any liability, loss or risk, personal or otherwise, which is incurred as a consequence, directly or indirectly, from the use or application of any contents of this book.

Any and all product names referenced within this book are the trademarks of their respective owners. None of these owners have sponsored, authorized, endorsed, or approved this book.

Always read all information provided by the manufacturers' product labels before using their products. The author and publisher are not responsible for claims made by manufacturers.

Paperback Edition

Manufactured in the United States of America

DEDICATION

This book is dedicated to all of you who give gifts from the heart and who know that giving your time to make a personal gift makes any gift a treasure. The true meaning of gift giving is in the feeling the giver and receiver share (my Mom taught me this!)..

Katie Cotton

CHAPTER 1- 9 EASY TO MAKE CHRISTMAS GIFT IDEAS FOR KIDS

The Christmas season is always the best time of DIY homemade gifts. It is fun to give toys that is something specifically tailored of the kids than their store bought toys. You can put together a huge ball pit or build them an a beautiful kiddie kitchen and those things are still played with nearly daily. Here are some of the wonderful DIY handmade gifts for kids this Christmas. And the best part about these gifts is that they work not only for this holidays, but also other special occasions.

SOFTEST PLAY DOUGH

Supplies
1 part Hair Conditioner
2 parts Corn Starch.
Food Coloring

Easy Homemade Christmas Gifts 2014

1. We added some food coloring for diversity. Since not all hair conditioners are the same consistency, you may need to alter the amounts just a bit so it is dough consistency.
2. Think of this as a mix between playdough and cloud dough. It is light and airy like cloud dough, but molds better as the conditioner helps the cornstarch become more pliable. You can also make goop or silly putty with cornstarch. It is such a fun ingredient to have in your craft cabinet!
3. You can make your Silky Play Dough as a gift for a friend. Package the playdough up with glitter, a couple of play dough toys (rolling pin, cookie cutters, sequins, etc.) and cupcake liners. Everything a princess needs for her own magical pretend play.

DRAWING JOURNAL

Materials Needed
Drawing paper
Thick paper for cover (watercolor paper, thin cardboard, or cardstock)
String or yarn
Hole puncher

1. Decide on the size of the journal and cut drawing paper and two cover pages to match. Make the cover pages slightly larger than drawing paper.
2. Decorate the cover. Cover the covers in pieces of bleeding tissue paper. Paint water over the tissue paper. Let it sit for a few minutes. Remove the tissue paper and let it dry.
3. Laminate or use clear contact paper on the covers.
4. Create three holes at the end of all paper and cover.
5. Attach the papers together with string. Tie loosely to allow room to move pages.

Enjoy giving a truly unique present to the special child in your life!

Katie Cotton
GREAT KEEPSAKE

Materials Needed
Model Magic
Colored Marker

1. Roll out your piece of Model Magic and push your child's hand in evenly.
2. Use a straw to make a hole in the top before it dries.
3. Let it dry for 24-48 hours, turn it over to make sure the back dries too.
4. Brainstorm some Christmas ideas of what could be drawn (eg. Snowmen.)
5. Now dried and ready for details! Use a black Sharpie to trace the outline of his hand.
6. Make sure you write your name and date on the back for posterity!

POPSICLE STICK PUZZLES

Materials Needed
Popsicle sticks
Crayons
Glue
Painters Tape

1. Tape the popsicle sticks together into a "canvas" of sorts. Use painters tape so the surface wouldn't get gummy.
2. Draw the outline of the picture you are going to create with permanent markers. Paint inside the lines of the pictures you drew.
3. Use shaving cream finger-paint as it doesn't spill. It's cheap, washable and smells nice.
4. To make the puzzles more difficult, wait until the paint dries, un-tape the sticks, mix them up and tape the painted side. Make a double sided puzzle – it is simple enough that the three year old kids could make them, but once you

mixed a bunch of the double-sided puzzles together, it is complicated enough to stump an 8 year old.

MELTING GIANT WAX CRAYONS

Use the crayon scraps to make your own crayons. This is a great way to use broken crayons and kids love doing this!

Melt crayons:
Hot plate
Small glass jars or bowls – an old muffin tin also works great!
Broken crayons – brands don't matter.
Candy mold – or ice cube trays.
Refrigerator or freezer space

Peel the crayon bits to remove the paper and sorting them into color groups. Melt the crayons in color groups. To melt you can either use a hot plate or melt it in the microwave in a bowl, inside a bowl of water. You want to be sure that it heats the wax evenly. Pour into the mold and then stick the mold into the fridge or freezer till the wax sets. Have fun!

CHRISTMAS SWEATER BABY LEG WARMERS

Supplies
Old Sweater
Scissors
Sewing Machine
Felt (1 sheet)
Needle and Thread (embroidery thread works best)

1. To start out, cut off the sleeves. If possible, try the leggings on your baby model to get an idea of the length.
2. Now that you have the length you want, cut off half of the sleeve cuff.

Katie Cotton

3. Take the cuff you just cut and pin it right sides together to the opposite end of the sleeve. Sew together with 1/4 inch seam.

4. Now you have one completed leg warmer. Follow those steps to finish your second leg warmer.

5. Grab your felt and cut out two little Christmas trees. You can use green felt Tip: Christmas trees are about 2 1/2 in x 3 in in size.

6. Pin the trees in place and grab a needle and thread to sew on the christmas tree patch. If you love the homemade look, stitch the tree patch. It didn't take any time at all to sew the trees on. Probably about 10 minutes for each tree. If you aren't crazy about hand stitching, you can use your sewing machine.

DIY DRUMS FOR YOUR LITTLE DRUMMER BOY

Supplies:
Tin cans
Leather
Decorative fabric
Leather laces
Crop-a-dile (or large needle)
Wooden dowel
Ball
Hot glue gun
Cotton.

1. Cut your fabric to fit around your tin can. Glue it in place.

2. Lay out your leather and trace around your can. Measure 1 inch around the traced circle and draw another circle.

3. Use a pen to map out your holes. Use a Crop-a-dile to punch the holes out. If you don't have a Crop-a-dile, you can use a large needle to make your holes.

4. Run your leather lace through the holes. Cinch tight over the top of the can. Repeat the same steps to the bottom. Run another leather lace diagonally through the top and bottom laces.

5. Insert your wooden dowel into the wooden ball. Glue cotton all over the ball to create your drum sticks.

6. Enjoy your adorable new gift!

COLORFUL JUGGLING BALLS

It is pretty easy to make good quality juggling balls and start learning how to juggle. The best thing about these juggling balls is the rubbery surface which gives them an excellent grip while learning to juggle. They can be decorated in many different ways.

> You will need:
> 9 balloons (makes 3 balls)
> Coffee Beans or Rice (dry, of course!)
> Scissors
> A cup of tea

Cut the tip off each balloon. Open up one balloon and pour in the coffee beans or rice until it is as full as it can get. Keep pressing down on it from all angles. This rearranges the beans or grains inside to create more space.

Now take another cut up a balloon and stretch it over the coffee filled balloon. Make sure you place it the other way around, so that the hole is facing the other side. This means the hole in the first coffee bean filled balloon is completely covered.

Now take a third balloon and do the same again, making sure the hole is facing another direction to the first and second. You can use the cut off pieces of balloon to decorate, or use a permanent marker to draw on them.

TOY SOAP

> Materials Needed:
> Small toy that will be of interest to your child
> Small piece of plastic wrap
> Glycerin (available at the craft store... I got mine for 50% off using a commonly occurring coupon)

Katie Cotton

> Soap mold or small plastic reusable snack container, silicone muffin cup, plastic baby food container, plastic container from snack sized yogurt or applesauce etc....
> Color (Optional): can use liquid food coloring or the stuff specific to soap making
> Essential oils or soap scent. Also available at a craft store.
> How to Create Play Soap:

1. Wrap toy tightly in a small piece of plastic wrap. It is best to choose a toy that won't be ruined if it gets damp, but the plastic wrap can be used to protect toys that can't sustain being soggy for extended periods or are at risk of being clogged by soap.
2. Following the instructions on the glycerin package melt a small amount in the microwave or using a double boiler. (it will about 2 min for 1 bar's worth to melt)
3. Add essential oils/color if desired.
4. Pour glycerin into the mold so it is 1/3 full (or 1/3 the depth of your bar of soap if using a container that is deeper than you want your soap to be)
5. Wait 5-10 min until glycerin has begun to set
6. Place toy upside down onto partially set glycerin.
7. Pour (re-melted) glycerin on top of toy until it is covered and to the depth you want your bar of soap to be.
8. Wait 30-40 min for soap to set and then pop out of the mold. You are ready to wash!!
9. Make treat soap as gifts for nieces and nephews (think Christmas presents, stocking stuffer etc.)

Easy Homemade Christmas Gifts 2014

CHAPTER 2- AWESOME DIY CHRISTMAS GIFT IDEAS FOR FRIENDS

Make this season merrier by crafting a handful of our best homemade Christmas gifts for your friend this year. Each Christmas gift idea is sure to wow your loved ones. They will adore these handy homemade Christmas gifts that are just as fun and easy to make as they are to give.

LOTION, NAIL FILE GIFT BOX

Create a box to hold a little lotion bottle and matching nail file.
Supplies
One 6 1/2" x 8" piece of heavy card stock for base
One 1 3/8" x 2 3/8" card stock for matting

Katie Cotton

    One 1 1/4" x 2 1/4" patterned paper for decorating
    1" Circle punch
    Scissors
    Paper trimmer
    Scoring tool
    Bone folder
    Sticky Strip, or other strong adhesive
    Patterned paper
    Stamps, and embellishments to decorate the completed box
    2 oz. bottle of hand lotion
    Coordinating nail file

1. Score the 6 1/2" x 8" piece of card stock at 2 1/2" and 4" on the 6 1/2" side.
2. Score the 6 1/2" x 8" piece of card stock at 2 1/2", 4", 6 1/2" on the 8" side.
3. Rotate cardstock 180 degrees so the 1 1/2" x 6 1/2" section is on the left. Snip off the left 1 1/2" x 2 1/2" upper and lower end flaps. Trim in between other flaps up to the center section.
4. Count four sections from left to right, trim the second and fourth flaps to a length of 1 1/2" to the nearest score line with a paper trimmer.
5. Punch small left 1 1/2" x 1 1/2" flap with 1" Circle punch.
6. Fold on score lines and assemble box with Sticky Strip. Fold middle flaps in first.
7. Decorate as desired.

HOMEMADE BEESWAX CANDLES

    Supplies:
    Beeswax
    Jars
    Candle wick
    Scissors
    Masking tape

Easy Homemade Christmas Gifts 2014

1. Begin by heating up the wax on the stove in a pot to 140°F. You don't want the temperature to exceed 185°F.
2. Pour a small layer into the base of a jar and place a piece of candle wick into the center of the jar
3. Hold this in place until the wax is dry enough to where the wick stays in place.
4. Next, make an X with tape over the top of the jar, poke a hole through the top and pull the wick through.
5. Fill up the jar with melted wax till the desired height.
6. After the wax is completely solid, cut the wick so that it's 1/2 inch tall.
7. Light + enjoy your pretty, new candles

DIY STUDDED PHONE CASE

What you'll need:
Phone case (I got 2 for $5 on Ebay)
Iron on the studs (make sure they have no "legs")
Krazy glue
Ruler
Pencil

1. Lay out your design first before gluing anything, just to get an idea of how it would look. When you have an idea of where the placement would be, remove all the studs, but one to mark the "start." Using a ruler, draw a line lightly with a pencil to use as a guide. Time to glue!
2. Put a small dot of glue directly onto the case, where you'd like the stud to go. Quickly place the stud on top of the glue. You can use a manicure stick to get the stud in the correct position as quickly as possible. As soon as you got the placement right, stopped touching it and moved on to the next one.
3. In order to maintain a straight line of studs, it's best to take your time. Take a break after a couple rows. Once you have all your studs glued, leave the case alone! No touching for at least 24 hours!

Katie Cotton
BEACH PHOTO JAR

Instructions:

1. Drill three holes on top of the jar lid. Note: This craft can be modified for any size jar. Smaller jars will need only one or two photos.

2. Mount photos onto chipboard of the same size with thread taped in between layers. Be sure to add a photo to the front and back since they will end up dangling and can spin around.

3. Add sand and shells to the bottom of the jar. Put a thread through holes in lid to desired photo height and tape off on top of lid.

4. Using Circle Cutter, cut circles of patterned paper to fit into the size of the lid. This easily covers up your thread and tape and provides a base for your star fish.

5. Emboss tan cardstock using the Dots Texture Plate and Texturing Tool. If desired, go back with stylus for more defined dots. Dab dots with white ink for extra pop.

6. Trim embossed cardstock to 4.5" square. Using Scoring Blade in Trimmer, score a line every 0.75" and fold accordion style, making sure the textured side is on the outside of your first fold. For smaller jars, cut 3" square and score every ½ inch.

7. Measure and staple at center of folded cardstock. Mark 0.5" from each side of staple and cut from that point to the opposing corner. Be sure to cut off from the open side, not the closed side.

8. Add adhesive between the mark and staple on each side of the star and fold out first pleat to meet and adhere to the other side. Repeat on opposite side. Fan out star evenly using the Stylus if needed to get into the folds. Adhere onto top of jar.

9. Print location and date onto blue cardstock and trim into rectangle. Mount onto white cardstock and cut around perimeter with Stamp Paper Edgers to add to the vacation theme.

10. Punch star from tan cardstock using Pop-up Star Punch. Place onto foam or mouse pad and punch several holes onto back using a pin and adhere onto tag.

Easy Homemade Christmas Gifts 2014

11. Punch hole into tag using 1/16 Inch Circle Hand Punch. Tie twine around the lid of the jar and attach a tag using jump ring to complete photo gear.

DIY PHOTO COASTERS

What You'll Need:

4x4 Tiles (I found mine at Lowe's for 16 CENTS a single tile, but I ended up buying a huge box of 80 of them for only $10 because I knew I would be making so many!)
Felt
Fabric Glue
Mod Podge
Sponge Brush
Acrylic Spray (Clear) (this makes the coaster water resistant so the photos don't get ruined or curled)

The reason this was SO EASY is because you don't have to cut or crop any photos to the 4x4 tile- Take any photo and cut/crop it into a 4x4 square!

1. Mod Podge the actual tile. This helps the photo adhere better to the tile.
2. Place the photo on the center of the tile IMMEDIATELY after the tile has been 'mod podged' so the photo adheres better. Then, cover the photo with mod podge. The mod podge will dry clear, just make sure you have an even coating and that all of the photo is covered. Again, this will help it adhere better and stay 'glued' to the tile. I did several coats, but waited for each coat to completely dry before adding another coat to make sure it didn't get all 'gloopy'.
3. Apply felt to the back of the tile. This will make sure the tile doesn't slip around on a surface or scratch it. Use tacky glue on the felt and just stuck it to the back of the tile! No need to specifically measure the felt, just kinda eyeballed' it.

4. Last and finally, 'waterproof' the coaster by spraying it with clear, acrylic, water resistant spray. This will make sure the coaster is water proof and keep the photo protected. You can use Krylon clear, glossy spray. Again, I did several coats of this, but waited for each coat to dry before applying a new one.

CRANBERRY LIME VODKA

1) Poke a hole in each of the cranberries with a sharp knife. It sounds labor intensive, but it's really not so bad. I poked holes in two bags worth of cranberries to begin with. Now, start to put the finished cranberries into your jar, but only fill up a third of the way.

2) Next, using a knife, peel off the lime rind and place them into your jar with your cranberries. Fill the jar up to the top with cranberries.

3) Next, you need to add a little bit of sugar to cancel out the bitterness of the cranberries. You don't want to make the vodka sweet, so add less than 2 tbsp of sugar to begin with {less if you have a small jar}. Now you can pour the vodka on top of the cranberry/lime/sugar mixture, seal the jar, and give it a good shake.

4) Give the jar a good shaking every day or two to make sure the sugar mixes throughout. You can let your infused vodka sit for anywhere from 2 weeks to 2 months. FYI: The longer you leave it the sweeter it'll be.

Note: To give away as gifts, pour the vodka into pretty jars and tie a ribbon or a gift tag on it. Add a cocktail-drink recipe tag to it to make it even more attractive. It makes amazing crantinis and also tastes great mixed with some club soda.

LET IT SNOW TREAT JARS

Supplies
- Glass bottles (I used these French square ones)
- Flocked vinyl

- Hole punch
- Clear window decal sheets (bought at an office supply store)
- Filler

1. Print out any image of your choice onto your window decal sheets and set aside.
2. Punch several dots out of your vinyl and put in a pile.
3. Peel off the backside of your vinyl dots and adhere all around the jar, leaving space for the decal.
4. Trim the decal to size and apply carefully trying not to touch the back with your fingers since it will smudge.
5. Fill with treats such as popcorn, granola, nuts or chocolates.

The good thing about these jars is that the dots and decal are easily removable so they can be reused for several purposes. Happy packaging!

CUPCAKE IN A JAR

You need small jars as many as you like
Ingredients:
- 2 1/2 cups all-purpose flour
- 1 1/2 cups sugar

Katie Cotton

- 1 tsp baking soda
- 1 tsp salt
- *2 1/4 tsp cocoa powder
- *1 1/2 cup canola oil
- 1 cup buttermilk, room temperature
- 2 large eggs, room temperature
- 2 tbsp red food coloring
- 1 tsp white distilled vinegar
- 2 tsp vanilla extract for the cream cheese frosting:
- 1 pound cream cheese, softened
- 2 sticks butter, softened
- 2 tsps vanilla extract
- 4 cups sifted powdered sugar

1. Batter is ready to be put in cupcake pan.
2. I spray the pan and then fill each hole up 2/3 with the batter. Note: I do not use liners, but you could if you want, just pull them off before putting them in the jar.
3. Usually they are done after about 17 minutes in my oven at temperature of 350 °F, and I take them out and put them on a wire rack to cool completely. Cool down
4. Once they are cool, I slice them in half. You will have a stack of tops and a stack of bottoms. Sliced in half
5. Place 1 bottom of each jar.
6. Put a layer of the frosting.
7. Take the top of the cupcake and place on top of the layer of frosting.
8. Flatten (gently smash) the top part of the cupcake inside the jar. You want to get the top sort of flat.
9. Beautifully frost the top of the cupcake.
10. Cover with lids and package, however you like! It will be heartbreaking to eat, as it is so pretty, but it is so yummy!

Easy Homemade Christmas Gifts 2014

CHAPTER 3- BEST HANDMADE GIFTS FOR MEN

We can see that there are a lot of crafts or handmade gifts out there to delight kids, girlfriends, sisters and mothers and yet, it is very hard to find really good handmade stuff for him, either to fathers, brothers or to special the man in our lives. This chapter is dedicated to them. Here are some good handmade gift ideas to inspire you to get crafty this Christmas.

INTERCHANGEABLE LEGO STAR WARS CLOCK

Materials:
Flat clay circle at least 12" in diameter - can also use wood
Print out of the death star from the internet

Katie Cotton

> *White paint - can be spray paint or anything that sticks*
> *Black and white paint*
> *Paintbrush*
> *Toothbrush*
> *Hanging wall clock kit with hands*
> *Permanent glue, gel consistency or epoxy*
> *12 2x4 flat lego bricks*
> *12 mini figs, Star Wars preferable, and accessories that go along with it*

1. Make the clock face and assemble clock mechanism. Make a flat 12 inch round clock face out of clay or buy one or make one out of wood, paint it white drill a hole in the center add the clock piece and glue it on.
2. Decorate the clock face. Cut out stencil of the death star and place over the clock make sure the stencil is away from the edge so that the legos don't block the view, mix some white and black paint together to get a light shade of gray, use a paintbrush and a toothbrush to splatter the gray paint over the stencil, mix a little more black in the gray and splatter some more, repeat until you get the effect you want, remove stencil and check out your work, add the clock hands and decorate, add the flat lego bricks at 12 o'clock, 1 o'clock, 2 o'clock, etc. until you have 12 pieces for each hour. Use a compass or protractor to be precise. 0 degrees and every 30 degrees around the circle. Or print out a template from the internet.
3. Add lego minifigures. Most will attach from the back of their legs, but if they don't add any extra pieces interchange at wil

MONOGRAM MUGS

Easy Homemade Christmas Gifts 2014

    Supplies
    Scissors
    Pen
    Tape
    Graphite transfer paper
    Black Pebeo Porcelaine Pen in Fine Point
    A printout with the his initials.

1. Cut out an initial and a piece of transfer paper. Tape the initial and the transfer paper (dark side down) to the mug.
2. Trace the initial. Any pen or pencil will work and experiment with different pressures to see what's best. Make a light outline. If you want, you can make your own transfer paper by rubbing a graphite pencil all over a sheet of plain paper.
3. Take your porcelain pen and trace over the lines of the initial. Get the edges nice and thick, then fill in with diagonal sketchy strokes.
- The sketchy strokes look best if they're all one direction
- It will help to have a blank paper handy where you can test the paint pen.
4. Once the lettering is done, let the mugs sit for 24 hours. Then bake them at 300 degrees for 35 minutes. It's fine to bake them with graphite residue. The graphite will wipe right off even after they're baked.
5. And that's it! Once they're baked, they're done. We pulled them from the oven, wiped them up and they were ready to go. For fun, we filled cellophane bags with hot cocoa mix and marshmallows and put them in the mugs.

Make a monogrammed mug for him with a Starbucks card inside. Or a matching 2-cup set for you and for him. Fun for Christmas, but equally fun for other events too.

Katie Cotton

KEYBOARD MESSAGE

Using an old computer keys to spell out a sweet message. Keyboard pieces are excellent for showing someone just how much you care. Not to mention, they work especially well as thoughtful gifts. A personal message always feels heartfelt.

>   What You'll Need:
>   Keyboard keys
>   Screwdriver
>   Frame
>   Letraset transfer letters (optional)
>   Glue gun

1. Use a screwdriver to remove your keys from an old keyboard.
2. Cover the keys with spray paint.
3. Stick on your Letraset letters. Or, just use a pen to write letters for yourself.
4. Remove the glass from your frame.
5. Hot glue your keys to the back of the frame.

This simple project allows you to customize the color as well as create duplicates of keyboard keys. Now you have the key to expressing your fondest feelings this Christmas.

JACK DANIEL'S SOAP DISPENSER

1. Buy a small bottle of Jack Daniel's, or another pretty bottle of liquor.
2. Transfer the liquor to another bottle
3. Buy a bottle of liquid soap - choose the fanciest pump you can find.
4. Pour soap into Jack Daniel's bottle and screw on the pump.

Easy Homemade Christmas Gifts 2014
Quick gift, right?

PHOTO BOOKMARK

Men who read a lot will give this gift a thumbs up.

>Supplies
>Grosgrain ribbon
>Scissors
>Needle
>Thread
>Photo
>Ribbon
>Tissue paper
>Book

1. Cut a piece of 2-inch-wide grosgrain ribbon 3 inches longer than twice the height of the book; snip a point at each end to prevent fraying.
2. Sew a 1 1/2-inch-by-2-inch photograph to the ribbon by hand-stitching each corner.
3. You might offer the bookmark with a new novel, wrapping the book with colored tissue paper and tucking the bookmark between two pages. Finish the gift with a simple ribbon or string.

UPCYCLED HANDLEBAR BAG

>You'll need
>A water bottle and an old sock that fits it and iron on reflective tapes.
>>Ribbon that can be ironed

1. Trim off the water bottle at the length you want.
2. Soften the opening by holding a lighter near to it, just enough to melt the very edge of the plastic.

3. Slip the sock over the bottle and position it the way you'd like it to end up.
4. Ensure that the sock hug the bottom end of the water bottle.
5. At the opening of the water bottle, allow a few inches to finish off the bag, and trim of the heel.
6. Close the bag with a draw string. Take the sock off the bottle and turn it inside out. Reinforce the edge of your sewing machine, then fold it in to make a channel for the ribbon.
7. Cut the ribbon and reflective tape long enough to wrap around the bottle, plus allow several inches to wrap around the handle bars and attach to the closure.
8. Trim the reflective tape before ironing it on. Iron on the tape according to the manufacturer's directions.
9. Take the bag outside and try out the length of the ribbon on the handlebars. Sew half the parachute buckle on one side, and make the other side to be adjustable. Attach the other parachute buckle by sewing Velcro to the ribbon.
10. The final step is to attach the ribbon to the sock. Did this in just one spot for each ribbon.
11. With the sock still on the bottle, slide a piece of ribbon under the sock to reinforce the back where you can sew the ribbon to the sock. Tack the ribbon in place on the outside. Slide the sock off the bottle, turn it inside out and finish attaching the ribbon.
Slide the sock back on the bottle and you're set.

LAPTOP DESK WITH A CHALKBOARD TO TAKE NOTES

Materials
Bent plywood stool, like the IKEA Benjamin
Saw
Two screws in towel hook

Easy Homemade Christmas Gifts 2014
    One extension cord
    Cable tacks

1. Decide on the height you'd like your riser. You could cut it long enough to allow you to place your legs under - breakfast in bed style - but that seemed a bit constricting for movie watching, so we cut our at around 4 inches. Place some masking tape on the cut line to prevent splintering, then cut with a saw.
2. Screw the two towel hooks on either end of one side, with the curved bottoms facing in.
3. Attach the extension cord to the inside with the cable tacks.
4. Then, just wrap the cable around the towel hooks for storage. And that's it!
You'll be amazed at what four inches and a flat surface will do in terms of view ability and security.

HAND PRINTED MOUSE PAD

Materials:
One 8" round mousepad blank (we got ours at Soft Expressions)
8 1/2 x 11" Full Sheet Labels
Computer and printer
Xacto or craft knife and cutting surface
Textile acrylic paint and stencil brush (both available at the craft store).
Iron and wax paper

1. Choose your design from one of the provided templates, or create your own. Print it out onto the label paper.
2. With your design in mind, decide on your color palette. You'll want to use a lighter color for the background, and a darker one for the foreground image. Pour out and your background paint onto a palette or scrape the surface, and use the stencil brush to create a base layer of color.

3. While this first coat dries, use the Xacto knife to cut out the gray shapes of the template.

4. Continue cutting your stencil until only the white shapes remain. Don't throw the smaller pieces away! These will be the resist for our the top layer of color
5. Peel the backing layer off the largest shape, and carefully place it on top of the mouse pad. Then, using the template as a reference, add the smaller shapes to recreate the full image on the mouse pad.
6. Mix up your top color, and using quick, consistent dabs, fill in the spaces with paint.
7. Once the paint has dried completely, cover the mouse pad with two layers of wax paper and iron on medium high (or follow the package directions) to help set the ink.

And, that's it – an easy way to add a little handmade warmth to even the most tech-heavy of workspaces.

Easy Homemade Christmas Gifts 2014

CHAPTER 4- FUN TO MAKE CHRISTMAS GIFTS IDEAS FOR GIRL FRIENDS

We all love to show our friends how much we love and appreciate them in some ways. We want them to know that they are very special to us and that they owned a special place in our hearts. Here are awesome Christmas gift Ideas you can make yourself that are sure to remind them of your friendship and how they complete your life. Hope this will help inspire you as these would be great for Christmas gift giving.

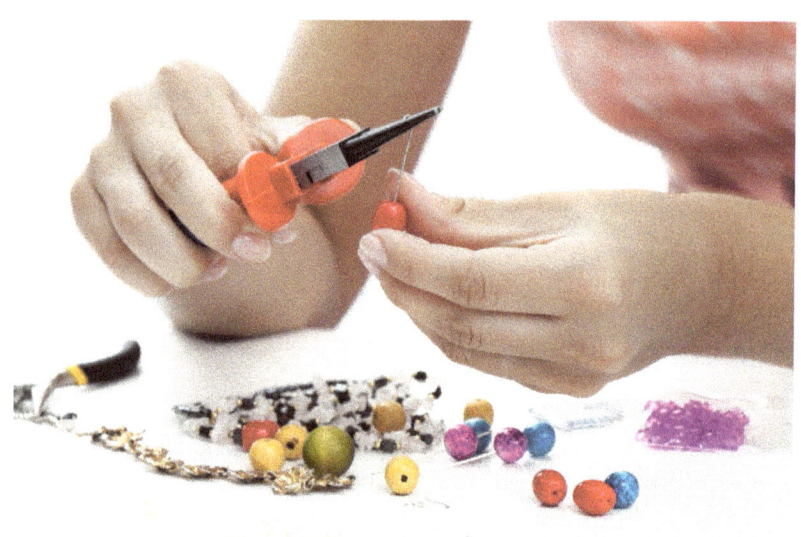

Katie Cotton
PERSONALIZED CANDLE
Making personalized candles is easier than you think. Today with some help from the kids we made some candles to give to my relatives and friends this Christmas season.

You will need:
Some regular paper
Tissue paper
Tape
Sharpies or markers
A candle
Wax paper
Heat gun

1 .Tape a piece of tissue paper, about the size of my candle, to a piece of copy paper. Markers will bleed through the tissue paper pretty easily so you will need something to protect your table, and it was easier for the kids to draw on the tissue paper when taped to the "paper".
2. Remove the tissue paper from the copy paper. Cut out your design, and place it onto your candle. It is important to cut away as much of the excess tissue paper as you can.
3. Next, take a piece of wax paper that is larger than your candle. Pull it tight around your candle, and use your heat gun to melt your design into the candle. Moving the heat gun in a back and forth motion for about 30-40 seconds. Be careful of your fingers, the heat gun will be hot.
4. Once you have heated the entire design gently peel back your wax paper and make sure the entire design is adhered to the candle. If not, just repeat with the wax paper and heat gun.

A very cute Christmas gift this Christmas. Don't you think?

SPA IN A JAR

In need of a little pampering, or know someone who is? Here's a super easy, inexpensive, yet very well received Jar gift idea suitable for many ages. This lovely spa jar contains . . .

A wide variety of spa items. Here are a few filler ideas for your own Spa jar:

- Trial size body lotions
- Mini soaps
- Facial masks
- Mini Manicure set
- A super soft scrub cloth
- Moisturizing lip balm
- Bath salts
- Chocolate Milk Bath
- Chocolate Milk Bath Bon Bons
- Chocolate Silk Coffee Scrub
- Cinnamon Swirl Coffee Scrub
- Fizzing Bath Bombs or Bath Oil Beads
- Peppermint Salt Foot Scrub
- A couple luxurious chocolates
- Cranberry Lip Gloss
- Energizing Foot Scrub
- Gingerbread Sugar Scrub
- Easy Bath Bags

OATMEAL BATH BOMBS

You'll Need:
- Mason Jar (wide mouth or regular, both work fine)
- A strip of scrapbook paper Or wrapping paper in a pretty design or Tissue Paper
- Print or hand-write a label for your jar

Simply wrap the strip around the jar (it's okay if it doesn't fit the entire way, you'll be adding a cute label anyways!)

Katie Cotton
Add your label, "Spa in a Jar"

Then carefully add your "ingredients" one item at a time. It's helpful to use the eraser end of a pencil to hold other items down, particularly if you're using a regular mouthed mason jar, rather than a widemouth jar.

POT HOLDER PURSE CADDY

What you'll need:
Rectangle hot pad
Needle & matching thread
Button
Snack size baggies
2 clothes pins
Sewing machine

Directions:
1. Fold the hot pad in half and sew a button on one side, making sure it matches up with the loop on the opposite side.
2. Place a snack size baggie on one side of the hot pad. Use clothes pins on each end to hold it in place. (The opening of the baggie needs to be along the outer edge of the hot pad.)
3. Sew the baggie. It best to sew the baggie's on one at a time. Do not try sewing more than one baggie at a time.

Once those are sewn, it's done! Just fill it with your purse essentials!

DIY PHOTO GIFT

Changed all photos to black and white to have consistency throughout the letter...

Materials: Scotch Tape (to tape the photos down). Make sure glue works too. Once the photos were all taped down, use Mod Podge as a sealant for the photos. Use a pretty generous amount. It's white but it will turn clear once it dries.

Place the photos along the letter. With your finger, press the photos down along the edge....

Cut. Tape. Repeat. Until you have a completed letter! Now it's time to mod podge the entire face of your letter to give it a nice finished look.

RIC RAC ROSE

Supplies
Ric Rac
Hot Glue
Any accessory to attach it to

1. Cut two pieces of Ric Rac at 21 inches or any length preferred. The Ric Rac, the taller the rose. The longer the Ric Rac, the wider the rose. To make some tiny ones, I would go with the smallest size Ric Rac.
2. Braid the two pieces of Ric Rac together. Keep going until you get to the end.
3. Take the end and curl the Ric Rac in.
4. Continue rolling the Ric Rac.
5. Put a little hot glue on the sides as you are rolling it. When you like the size of your rose, you can stop rolling.
6. Put a little glue where you want to end the Ric Rac and cut the excess off. Then glue the tails securely under the rose.
7. Pull the edges of the Ric Rac down. Keep pulling the Ric Rac edges down until you like how it looks.
8. Your Ric Rac rose is ready to be attached to any available accessories you wish. Put quite a bit of hot glue on the base part. Then attach your Ric Rac rose.
9. Let it dry for a bit, push the edges of the rose down over the base to make it a little flatter.

Katie Cotton
TEACUP CANDLES

You will need:
Glue Gun
Candle Thermometer or candy thermometer
Pre-waxed Wire Wick with clip
Creme Wax and or pieces of old candle from your home
Bag clippers or bamboo sticks
Scent for Candles (you can do rose, vanilla, lavender, etc)
Vintage Silver Containers or tea cups
or any other container you like
Double boiler
The important thing is that the water is not supposed to touch the glass container.

1. Set the double boiler with water, cut wax and place it inside the container. Hook on the thermometer. Burner on high.
2. Glue the wire core wick clip using the glue gun at the bottom of the containers you are using.
3. Hang wick by off a bamboo stick so that the wick is nice and straight. You can also use a bag sealer clip to grab wick, it just needs to be long enough.
4. Once the wax is melted and gets to about 180F, take it out of the stove and add color. Wait until it gets to 175F and add scent.
5. Pour the wax into each container making sure the wick stays in place.
6. Let it sit a little and then i added the rose petals so they sited at the top.
7. Check them for the next half an hour on and off to make sure the wick was still in place...
...... And voila fabulous candles in literally an hour or less!!!

CHAPTER 5- UNDER 5 DOLLARS DIY CHRISTMAS GIFT IDEAS

Bare in mind that handmade items are not just beautiful, but special... There's something extra special about homemade gifts. The flashy and expensive gift has no room in the habitat of friendship. Who knows... you may be able to make some of these for free if you have all the supplies on hand.

HOMEMADE LEMON SOAP

Supplies:
1 1/2 cups Goat's milk soap base, cubed
4-6 Lemon essential oil
Dried Lemon zest of 3-4 lemons

1. Cut soap into cubes and microwave in 30 second intervals (use a large Pyrex measuring cup to melt the soap in). This recipe makes 3 bars of soap and I used about 15 cubes of goat's milk soap base.
2. Melt soap for about a minute. Add another 15-30 seconds if it's not completely melted.
3. Once soap cubes have liquified add a few drops of the lemon essential oil and the lemon zest; stir well.
4. Pour into soap molds and allow to harden for at least one hour. Press mold to release the soap.

IPAD KITCHEN TABLET HOLDER

Supplies
Old cutting board
Scrabble tile holder
Child's building block.
Wood glue
White paint

1. Glue and attach the Scrabble tile holder to the bottom front of the cutting board.
2. Glue the building block at the back of the cutting board.
3. Paint the holder white, sand the edges and then stain the piece.

JAR LID PICTURE MAGNETS

Supplies
Gloss Mod Podge
Dimensional Magic Mod Podge
Images or pictures
Brush
1 Box of Lids.
Scissors or Circle Puncher
Magnets

Easy Homemade Christmas Gifts 2014

1. Print pictures on white card stock.
2. The size of your pictures will depend on the size of the lids you are going to use.
3. Get a wide mouth lid size for your magnets.
4. Use a 3" circle punch to trim my photos. It is the perfect size for this project.
5. Center the image where you want it and then punch it.
6. Paint the beige inside part of the lid with the Gloss Mod Podge. The red part of the lid will become the magnet's frame.
7. Place your image on top of the lid and smooth out any bubbles using your fingers.
8. Add another coat of Gloss Mod Podge on top of the picture and let it dry.
9. The last step is to apply a layer of Dimensional Magic on top of the picture.

It will look weird while wet, but after it dries it will give your magnets a beautiful smooth dimensional glossy finish that you'll love.

Let them dry overnight or for a full 24 hours before you add the magnets to the back of the lids.

SNOW GLOBE NECKLACE

Supplies
1 small bottle brush Christmas tree (found at most craft stores),
1 small glass bottle pendant
Jewelry chain
Jump ring
Glitter
Hot glue gun
Glue
Toothpick
Wire cutters
Round nose pliers.

Katie Cotton

1. Use your wire cutters to trim the tip of the tree (put your jar next to your tree to determine how much you need to trim off.)
2. Put a glob of hot glue on the tip of your toothpick and carefully put the hot glue on the inside bottom of your jar. Put your tree in immediately to secure, using the toothpick to position it properly. Let dry.
3. Carefully fill your jar with glitter.
4. After you've poured the glitter in, put some hot glue on your cork and insert into the bottle to seal.
5. Add your jump ring and chain.
Now you have a perfect little snowy world in miniature.

LEAF-IMPRINTED CLAY NECKLACE

Supplies
Small leaves
Polymer clay and roller, possibly a clay cutter depending on your design idea
Jump ring and chain
Optional acrylic paint and sealer (like Sculpey Gloss Glaze)

1. Roll the clay out to about 1/4 inch.
2. Press your small leaf into the clay, vein side/backside toward the clay, then flip your clay over and roll it out a little. The reason for flipping it over is so your leaf can't move. Do not try to roll your clay out any flatter here – it will break your leaf apart and make it harder to remove.
3. Peel your leaf off. Just a little extra work to gently remove all the pieces.
4. Trim your clay to the size pendant you want. I opted for a 1 – 1/2 inch circle.
5. When cutting it, go for an offset look. You can center yours is you like.
6. Poke a hole in your pendant with a toothpick and lay it on a baking sheet.

Easy Homemade Christmas Gifts 2014

7. Bake it according to the package instructions. This will vary by brand, but what you can expect is that it will take about 30 minutes for each 1/4 inch thick your pendant is in a low-temperature oven.

8. Once it's baked and cooled, add some paint.

9. With a bit of damp paper towel, I wiped off the excess paint from the surface, leaving the paint just in the leaf veins. If you wipe off too much, just try again.

10. Add some Sculpey Gloss if you want to seal it with a shiny finish, but that's totally optional.

11. When it's dry, just add a jump ring and chain.

Now you can wear a little bit of nature!

SHOWER CURTAIN RING BRACELETS

Large Shower Curtain Ring
Fabric scraps (the prettier, the better)

1. Cut strips of fabric about 1/2" wide.

2. Hot glue one end of the fabric to the inside of the shower curtain ring.

3.Start wrapping the fabric tightly around the ring adding small amounts of glue as you go.This will help the fabric stay in place.

3. When you get to the end cut the remain fabric and glue it to the inside of the ring. You can add small ornamements as well-glue them on or attach like a charm

4. These can be amazingly pretty and original. It all depends on your choice of fabric and imagination. I used green leather strips and wound silver colored wire over the leather

ADJUSTABLE RIBBON BRACELET

MATERIALS
Ribbon
Embellishments
Jewelry wire

1. Fold about 3/4 of a yard in half. Don't cut it. Fold the ribbon and get your pins. Hold the folded halves together, pinning right in the middle of the ribbon.
2. After pinning sew both edges together, leaving the center empty.
3. Sew all the length of the ribbon as close to the edge as you can.
4. Get the wire and bend the end of it so it is not sharp. Using pliers squish the top together to make it flat and smaller.
5. Cut the end of the wire when you get to the end.
6. Using your fingers push the ribbon back, making it ruffle.
7. Fold the wire making a loop and squish it with the pliers.
8. With hot glue, seal the other end of the ribbon.
9. To keep the ruffle secure and in place, fold each end of the bracelet one more time.
9. Use any embellishment you like.
10. Hot glue your embellishments in place.

We are done! The best thing about this bracelet is that it would fit anyone since you can adjust it.
Isn't that awesome!

YARN WRAPPED CANDLES

Supplies
LED pillar candles
Yarn in your choice of colors
Hot glue gun
Scissors

1. Put a dab of hot glue on the candle where you want to start wrapping the yarn and press the end of the yarn into it.
2. Start wrapping the yarn around the candle, pulling taut and using your thumb to push the yarn rows close together so there are no gaps in between rows.
3. When you have the yarn band as wide as you want it, cut the yarn and adhere with another dab of hot glue. Repeat with another color if you want.

It literally takes just a few minutes to wrap the yarn around the candles and give them a whole new look for fall. These would be fun on a mantel, as a table centerpiece, or on your outdoor patio.

Katie Cotton

CHAPTER 6- 15 CUTE HOMEMADE GIFTS, KIDS CAN MAKE

There is nothing much nicer than a homemade Christmas gift from a special child in your life and if you can encourage the kids to make presents for their friends, teachers, grandparents they will be treasured forever.

HANDPRINT SNOWMAN ORNAMENT

Supplies
Plain ornament, acrylic paint (white plus any other colors of your choosing) and a paint brush

Paint the palm of one of your girl's hands white. Have her hold the bottom of the ornament with her painted hand -- just make sure she doesn't squeeze too tight! After she releases her hand gently, you will see finger marks that look like snowmen! Use the paintbrush to add details like eyes, a carrot nose, top hats and scarves. Give one to everyone in your snowman clan.

Easy Homemade Christmas Gifts 2014

SNOW GLOBE JAR

Supplies
A glass jar, hot glue gun, Lego pieces (or any figurine), glitter and water

Hot glue the Legos or figurines to the lid of the jar and let dry. Then add a plastic tree (from a toy set or the craft store) to make the snow globe more holiday-themed. Then your kid can fill up the jar with water and add colorful glitter. Take the lid, turn over, and screw onto the jar for your kid. Then, shake, shake, shake for a winter wonderland! So cute -- and super easy.

PICTURESQUE CORKBOARDS

Supplies
Embroidery hoops, foam, cork backing, glue, pencil, painters tape, paint and paint brushes

Using the inside of the hoop, trace the outline of a circle on the cork backing roll as well as the foam. Cut out the circles and glue together. Once dry, glue into the embroidery hoop. Then let your guy paint designs -- geometric like this one or not -- onto the cork board. Let dry. Use a thumbtack to hang a picture of the cousins -- and your boy can gift away!

POLKA DOT FLOWER VASE

Supplies
Empty glass bottles or mini-vases, dot labels (get them at the office supply store), ribbon, scissors and double-sided tape

Have your kid decorate the vase with the dot labels. Next, measure the width of the base of the vase with ribbon and cut to fit, leaving a little extra to ensure it'll make it all the way around. Then have your kid take the double sided tape and secure the ribbon -- or they can tie it instead. Then your kid can add more ribbon or

Katie Cotton

polka dots to finish his masterpiece. This makes a perfect holiday gift for his teacher -- just add flowers!

DIY PAPERWEIGHT

Supplies

1/4 cup of salt, 1/4 cup of water, 1/2 cup of flour, a bowl, a cookie sheet and pebble gravel

Preheat your oven to 250 degrees. Have your gal take the salt, water and flour and mix together thoroughly in the bowl to create the dough. Roll her creation into a ball and flatten out on the cookie sheet. Then, she can take the pebbles and spell out a special message for Dad (or whoever is left on her shopping list). Bake in the oven for two hours or until dry and stiff, then let it cool afterwards overnight. It's the perfect paperweight!

PINWHEEL NECKLACE

Supplies

Wooden washer (available at your local craft store), lanyard of any color, wood paint and a paint brush

Have your girl paint a pretty design on the wooden washer -- which will now be a fashionable new pendant. Then let dry and loop the lanyard through the hole and tie at the ends. Easy! Wrap in a decorative box and give to big sis!

WOODEN BEADED NECKLACE

Supplies

String or yarn, scissors, wooden beads, painter's tape, paint and a small paintbrush

Using painter's tape, tape around one half of the bead -- this will ensure you have nice, even paint lines. Do this for all of the beads. Then let your kid paint the beads, however they'd like. Once dry, help them string the beads onto the yarn and cut to the desired length.

Easy Homemade Christmas Gifts 2014

HANDPRINT TREE APRON

White apron, fabric paint, paintbrush, hands

Start with the biggest hands in the family (cue mom and dad). Paint hands green and place handprints (fingertips pointing toward bottom hem) across base of the apron. As the tree tapers, use smaller and less handprints. Cover thumbs with other paint colors to create thumbprint ornaments and decorations.

CUSTOMIZED TRAY

Supplies

Wooden breakfast tray, paints, paintbrush, favorite photos or magazine images, stickers

Set your child up with trays and paints, and let her go to town. Once dry help her glue on photos, magazine images and stickers.

HANDY COASTERS

Supplies

Cardstock, pencil or chalk, 2 fabrics in coordinating patterns, 1 package double-sided stiff fusible interfacing, iron

Trace hand on cardstock and cut out to use as your template. Using pencil or chalk, trace the template on one of the patterned fabrics. Cut a rectangle of fabric that includes the tracing. Cut the second patterned fabric, as well as the interfacing, into the same rectangular size. Iron both fabrics and interfacing together (as per the interfacing package's instructions) and cut out the traced hands.

BEAUTIFUL BOTTLE PRINTS

Supplies

Acrylic or fabric paint, disposable plates, paintbrush, small plastic bottle (partly filled with water), stampable item such as craft paper or canvas tote

Katie Cotton

> *Pour small pools of paint onto plates, using one plate per color. Dip the bottom of the bottle into paint and stamp bottle firmly onto craft paper or tote bag. Once dry, you'll have yourself a signature wrapping paper or tote bag.*

PICTURE FRAME ORNAMENT

> *Supplies*
> *Construction paper, glue stick, scissors, photo, ribbon, tape, decoration (e.g. Markers, glitter, craft foam pieces), picture frame ornament template*

Print and cut out picture frame template. Fold construction paper in half. Place template on construction paper, lining up one side of the picture frame to the folded edge of construction paper. Trace frame and trim away the edges. Cut out the center (be sure to only cut hole in the top flap of construction paper) -- this will be where the photo appears. Decorate the frame with markers and glitter. Insert photo and seal open edges of frame with glue.

VOTIVE CANDLE HOLDERS

> *Supplies*
> *Clear glass votive candle-holder, colored rock sugar, glue*
> *Coat candle-holder with glue, then sprinkle with colored sugar. Dry.*

EMBROIDERED FELT PURSE

> *Supplies*
> *Felt, needle and thread, yarn*

Cut a square of felt in half. Fold one of the halves, leaving a 2" tab that will serve as the top flap, then stitch both sides closed. Pencil in a simple design on a purse, then embroider along the pencil lines. Sew button onto the flap. For strap, braid yarn (or knit a cord) and sew onto the purse.

FABRIC NECKLACE

Supplies
Stretchy rag, large beads, scissors, needle nose pliers

Take a stretchy rag (like old sweatpants) and cut out a 24" x 2" strip. String beads along strip, space accordingly and tie ends together.

Katie Cotton

CHAPTER 7- 5 LOVELY GIFTS YOU CAN MAKE FOR YOUR GRANNIES

Grandparents are the most difficult to shop, probably it's because at this point in their lives, there isn't much that they actually need or want. But most Grannies want for Christmas is simple....They only want memories of their grandkids. Here are some easy, crafty gifts will make any Grannies smile at Christmas.

SALT DOUGH HANDPRINT ORNAMENT

4 cups of Flour
1 cup salt
Food coloring
Large Mixing Bowl
Water to moisten
Cookie sheet
Just a tad of oil
A small rolling pin or wooden dowel
A drinking straw

Easy Homemade Christmas Gifts 2014

    Ribbon

    A plate for a guide

    *Paint *if desired*

1. In your mixing bowl ~ gradually blend in your flour & salt with water.Remember to add gradually, because you can always add more water than take away.

2. Lightly grease my baking sheet with oil & form & roll out on the cookie sheet. 3. Once you have your form mode, use a straw to make a hole in it before you have your kids emboss their hand print.

3. Keep in mind you need to have your dough thick enough to form the handprint. If your dough is too thin, it will not work. Place in a 150* degree oven for an hour. Or you can air dry over night & for 24 hours.

4. Paint or gloss, however you'd like.

There's nothing better than homemade ornaments.

A CHRISTMAS GIFT FOR GRANDMA

    Picture Frame

    8x10 (Find words that best describe your Grandma and print)

    Butterfly stickers

1. Insert print in frame
2. Attach butterflies to the left of each description under (or over whichever you like better) the glass

And that's it. Super easy, right??

GRANDMA BLOCKS

    Painted wood blocks

    Vinyl

    Mod Podge

1. Cut the blocks down to 3.5 in. For the base cut to 7 inches.
2. Give each block a couple coats of paint

Katie Cotton

3. Print out the vinyl with Silhouette. You could really do any variation of colors. Chose a more neutral color to match their houses.
4. Distressed the edges with a little distress ink.
5. Cut pictures down to 3×3 and modpodged them on.
6. Once they were dry, tie a little bow around them, and sent them off to grandma's!

MOD PODGED ORNAMENTS

Supplies
Wooden ornaments
Spray paint, or craft paint
Scrapbook paper
Mod podge and foam brush
Ribbon
Vinyl lettering, or other embellishments (Christmas shapes, etc.)

1. Paint your ornaments--both sides, and let dry completely. If you can't find wooden ornaments with the holes, just use a drill to make your own holes. You could also use any shape you like!
2. Trace the ornament onto the back side of your scrapbook paper, then cut out.
3. Trace the ornament hole, then use a hole punch or exacto knife to remove the center.
4. Mod podge the paper onto the front side of your ornament, and let dry completely.
5. Sand the edges of the ornament, removing any excess paper along the edges.
6. Add your vinyl, or other embellishments. I used black vinyl-- century gothic font.
7. Tie on your ribbon!

COUNT YOUR BLESSINGS BOARD

SUPPLIES:
- Bead board/Wood
- Hard board
- Saw
- Scrapbook Paper
- Mod Podge
- Foam Brush
- Vinyl
- Paint
- Small Clothespins
- Embellishments

1. Cut your bead board to approximately 12 inches x 20 inches. And your hardboard into 4 pieces that are approx. 4.5 x 6.5 inches. You will also need one hardboard piece that is approx. 2.5 inches x 12 inches.
2. Paint your beadboard piece and let dry.
3. Cut out 4 pictures of your children that are approx. The same size of your 4 rectangular pieces. Mod Podge these on to the rectangles and let dry. Cut out a new piece of scrapbook paper that will go into the long rectangular piece. Mod Podge this on as well.
4. Distress beadboard and hardboard if desired.
5. Hot glue all 5 rectangular pieces to your beadboard.
6. Add vinyl to rectangular piece
7. Add ribbon to back. I used wood for the sample instead of bead board and to add vinyl,marked the center on the back and then marked a spot 3 inches on either side. Staple the ribbon to the back using my staple gun and then tied a knot. For the bead board drill holes through the top and had them strung the ribbon through.
8. Now add embellishments and hot glue mini clothespins to the tops.

Katie Cotton

And what's best is depending on the paint or scrapbook paper and embellishments each board is so personalized and different!

HANDPRINT TREES WRAPPED CANVAS

12"x24" canvas (perfect size for three hands, grab a smaller size for one or two)
Piece of burlap
Scraps of fabric for handprint trees and flower blossoms
Hot glue gun
Iron on adhesive

1. Trace your child's hand and part of their arm on the paper side of your iron-on adhesive.
2. Iron the Heat n Bond with the handprint onto the wrong side of your tree trunk fabric. Then cut out your tree trunks and set aside.
3. Cut out your burlap to be slightly larger than your canvas. You'll want it large enough to wrap around the sides and onto the back.
4. Wrap your burlap around the canvas. Put a small line of hot glue on the back edge of the canvas, pulled the burlap tight and pressed it onto the glue (using a spoon so the hot glue didn't seep through the holes in the fabric and burn!) fold over any excess burlap on the back and glued it down to finish the back a little more.
5. Peel the paper backing off your handprints and iron them in place on the burlap. It actually worked quite well, put a potholder under the open part of the canvas to press up and make a more solid surface to press the iron down on.
6. Now, get to work cutting out your cherry blossoms. For the petals, cut out some puffy, plus sign shapes and then smaller circles of the darker pink and white colors.
7. To make the blossoms, use a squirt and smush technique. Squirt a bit of hot glue on the dark pink circle, then bunch up and smash on the white circle. Then, squirt a bit more hot glue in the

Easy Homemade Christmas Gifts 2014

center of your petals, put your counters in place, then smash and pinch the back part to make your blossom three dimensional.

8. Begin hot gluing your blossoms onto your tree. Keep going until they are filled with the pretty blossoms.

9. And you're finished! You have a pretty Spring wall hanging that captures your child's handprints from this year.

Katie Cotton

CHAPTER 8- 10 TOTALLY DO-ABLE DIY CHRISTMAS GIFT IDEAS USING MASON JARS

Everybody loves the classic mason jar? We can't deny both its utility and inherent cuteness. We trust it to preserve all of our favorite food. But did you know that these jars can be used for more than just canning? Now, discover some clever ways to re-purpose a mason jar that you just can't keep to yourself and how amazing they can be as Christmas gift ideas!

CHRISTMAS CANDIES GIFT JAR

Supplies
Mason Jar or any jar
Twine, ribbon or jute
Printable Tag
Christmas Candies

Easy Homemade Christmas Gifts 2014
>Paint
>Stencils
>Dauber Set

1. Gather your supplies.
2. Paint the top of your lid and let dry.
3. Use your stencil to paint on a Christmas Shape. (e.g. Christmas trees or snowflake) Let dry.
4. Print and cut some printable tags.
5. Tie your printable tag around the rim of your jar.
6. Place your Christmas candies on the jar and twist jar lid on.

Voila!! Now you have a super cute way to hand out some fun and festive cupcake treats in an inexpensive but cute way!

MASON JAR CANDY PEDESTALS
>Supplies
>3 mason jars, in varying heights (You could also use clean pickle or other jars if you'd prefer)
>3 lids & lid rings
>3 glass candlesticks (from the dollar store)
>Hot glue (optional)
>Glue
>Spray paint
>Chalkboard paint (optional)

1. Lightly spray paint your lids and candlesticks; allow to dry, then spray again. Repeat until covered. It is best to glue the lids to the mason jar rings before or after spraying.
2. After your candlesticks have dried completely, squirt some of the glue on the base of your mason jars, let sit for 30 seconds, then set the candlestick in place. Be sure to get it centered or your jar will sit crooked.
3. Let dry for 24 hours!
4. (Optional) Paint the tops of your lids with chalkboard paint to give it a little something extra.
5. Fill your jar with lots of Christmas candies.

Katie Cotton
PERSONALIZED MASON JAR DRINK

Supplies
Mason jar
Scrapbook paper in your choice of color and design
Chipboard letters in your choice of color and design
Burlap ribbon
Craft glue
Scissors

1. Begin by cutting a length of burlap ribbon to fit the mason jar. Wrap the burlap around the jar, snip, and glue it in place.
2. You now want to cut a strip of scrapbook paper that is half the width of the burlap ribbon. This will create a layered look. Cut the paper, wrap, and secure it with glue as well.
3. Use a chipboard letter to personalize the mason jar. We used one letter, but you can use all three initials of the person's name if you wish. This is a great way to add a personal touch and be sure that none of your guests get their drinks mixed up!

Once the glue is dry on your ribbon, scrapbook paper, and chipboard letter. Your mason jar now has tons of personality and is ready to party.

Easy Homemade Christmas Gifts 2014

DIY LAVENDER BATH SALTS

Supplies

Mason Jar

2 cups epsom salts

10-20 drops lavender essential oil

1. Add the epsom salts to a mixing bowl and break up any clumps.
2. Stir in the essential oils.
3. Store in a mason jar in a cool place.

This would make a great homemade Christmas gift!

DIY PEPPERMINT SUGAR SCRUB

Supplies

Mason Jar

2 cups organic cane sugar

1 cup grapeseed oil (or coconut, olive, or almond oil)

20-30 drops peppermint essential oil

1. Add the sugar to a mixing bowl.
2. Gradually pour in the oil and stir to combine. You may not need the full cup of oil - you want just enough to moisten all of the sugar without it being too oily.
3. Add in your essential oil and mix well.
4. Store in a Mason Jar in a cool place.

DIY LUXURIOUS HOMEMADE WHIPPED BODY BUTTER

Supplies

1 cup coconut oil, solidified

10-15 drops of your favorite essential oil* (optional)

1. Add the coconut oil to your electric stand mixer.
2. Whip at a high speed until the oil becomes light and fluffy (about 5 minutes).
3. Add your oils and mix well. (optional)
4. Store in a mason jar in a cool place.

Katie Cotton

Notes
Great oils to use include lavender, frankincense, myrrh, and sweet orange. Use caution if you choose a citrus oil as it could cause photo sensitivity.
If your oil liquifies (coconut oil melts at temperatures above 76º) you can pour it back into your mixer and whip it again.

SNOWY MASON JAR

Supplies
Glue
Epsom Salt
Mason Jars
Brush
Optional: twine, Christmas picks

1. Begin by covering the jar with decoupage glue.
2. Cover the entire jar with epsom salt. This will make the jar appear like its covered in snow. It also looks beautiful when a candle is lit.
3. Tie twine around the mouth of the jar and hot glue mixed berries and picks.

A simple and easy to make mason jar craft that's perfect for the holiday season.

MASON JAR SNOW GLOBE

Mason jar or any jar that seals
Distilled Water
Liquid Glycerin
Glitter
Figurines
Epoxy/Crazy Glue

1. Using the Crazy Glue, attach your figurines to the lid of the mason jar. Let them dry completely. (Wait for 24 hours to be sure.)

2. Fill your jar almost to the top with distilled water. Add a dash of liquid glycerin (this is used to make the glitter fall more slowly). The amount is glitter you add is sort of at your own discretion. I ended up experimenting and some of mine have a lot of glitter and some don't. . Screw the cap on tightly and shake your jar to get the glitters moving.

And you're done! Give your Christmas decorations a pretty handmade touch this year

A GORGEOUS MASON JAR CANDLE

Supplies
Mason jar
Two large pillar candles
A wick
A large pot
Oven mitts
Tape

How To Make It:
1. First, cut your jar in half using a glass-cutting kit.
2. Wearing oven mitts, light the yarn on fire. Rotate the jar so that the entire string is lit.
3. After 40 seconds or so, dunk the jar in ice water. It should split into two around where the string is tied.
4. Tap the jar back together where it splits.
5. Melt your two candles in a pot over the stove.
6. Dip the bottom of your wick in the hot wax and stick it to the bottom of the jar.
7. Pour the hot melted wax into the jar. Keep the jar in ice water (make sure the wax doesn't get wet) to help the wax set.
8. When the wax has completely cooled, remove the tape and pull the jar off your candle.

Katie Cotton
MASON JAR SOAP DISPENSER

Supplies
Old soap bottle (with pump)
2 Part Epoxy
Drill with hole attachment
Scissors or boxcutter
Marking pen

1. Cut off top of the old soap bottle just below the thread
2. Use pen to measure and mark a circle in the lid of the mason jar
3. Drill hole in lid of mason jar
4. Mix epoxy and apply to the lower rim of the bottle top
5. Insert the pump dispenser through the bottle top and screw tightly to secure
6. Let the epoxy dry according to the instructions
7. Fill with your favorite liquid soap

Easy Homemade Christmas Gifts 2014

CHAPTER 9- HOMEMADE DOG-I-Y TREAT RECIPES

Christmas is the best time to bake dog biscuits for all the dogs in our family plus the dogs owned by a few friends and neighbors. These biscuits are a healthy everyday treat, and useful for a dog with a sensitive stomach, or minor digestion issues. If your dog is showing any signs of serious distress, remove all food and contact your veterinarian immediately.

PEANUT BUTTER DOGGIE TREATS
Recipe from BrownEyedBaker.

> Ingredients:
> 1 cup whole-wheat flour
> 1/2 Tablespoon baking powder
> 1/2 cup natural peanut butter

Katie Cotton

    1/2 cup low-fat milk

Preheat oven to 375 degrees. In a bowl, combine flour and baking powder. In another small bowl, mix peanut butter and milk. Add wet mixture to dry, and mix well.

Turn out dough on a lightly floured surface and knead. Roll out to 1/4-inch thickness and cut out shapes. Place on a baking sheet lined with parchment paper and bake 12 – 15 minutes or until lightly brown. Cool and store in an airtight container.

PUMPKIN DOG BISCUITS

    2 eggs
    1/2 cup canned pumpkin
    2 Tbsps dry milk
    1/4 tsp sea salt
    2 1/2 cups brown rice flour *
    1 tsp dried parsley (optional)

Preheat oven to 350.

In large bowl, whisk together eggs and pumpkin to smooth. Stir in dry milk, sea salt, and dried parsley (if using, optional). Add brown rice flour gradually, combining with spatula or hands to form a stiff, dry dough. Turn out onto lightly floured surface (can use the brown rice flour) and if the dough is still rough, briefly knead and press to combine.

Roll dough between 1/4 – 1/2" – depending on your dog's chew preferences, ask first – and use biscuit or other shape cutter to punch shapes, gathering and re-rolling scraps as you go. Place shapes on cookie sheet, no greasing or paper necessary. If desired, press fork pattern on biscuits before baking, a quick up-and-down movement with fork, lightly pressing down halfway through the dough. Bake 20 minutes. Remove from oven and carefully turn the biscuits over, then bake additional 20 minutes. Allow to cool completely on rack before feeding to the dog.

Makes up to 75 small (1") biscuits or 50 medium biscuits
Christmas Candies Gift Jar

BACON DOG BISCUITS

>   1 1/2 cups whole wheat flour
>   1 cup all-purpose flour
>   1 cup skim milk powder
>   1/3 cup bacon drippings
>   1 large egg
>   1 cup cold water

1. Combine both flours and milk powder in large bowl.
2. Drizzle with fat. Add egg and cold water.
4. Mix well to form dough {if the dough is too sticky, add flour until it reaches a suitable consistency for rolling}.
5. Turn out onto a lightly floured surface.
6. Roll out to 1/2 inch thickness.
7. Cut with bone-shaped cookie cutters.
8. Place on an ungreased baking sheet and bake at 300 degrees for 60 minutes.

Makes about 3 dozen cookies, depending on the size of the cookie cutter. Package them in a bag with some cute ribbon and be prepared for a whole lot of dog appreciation!

SWEET POTATO DOG CHEW TREATS

>   Ingredients:
>   Large sweet potatoes
>   Mandoline or sharp knife
>   Cutting Board
>   Baking Sheets

Katie Cotton
> Aid of your choosing for greasing the pans
> Oven

Directions:
Preheat oven to lowest setting; ours went all the way down to 175 degrees. Meanwhile, slice one top of sweet potatoes to make for easier balancing when slicing. Carefully cut thick lengthwise slices of the sweet potato using a sharp knife or mandoline, about 1/3 inch thick for larger chews. Make them thick — when dehydrating, the slices are going to lose the majority of their thickness.

Grease your baking sheets and arrange slices on a flat surface of pans. Place pans on the top racks inside oven.

Let it slowly cook and dehydrate over a period of about 8 hours.

This process is a great way to make natural, gluten free and grain free treats for your dogs— and save a little money while you're at it!

HOMEMADE FLAX SEED DOG BISCUITS

> *Ingredients:*
> 12 oz whole wheat flour
> 12oz bread flour
> 2 oz wheat germ
> 1 tsp salt
> 2 Tbsp brown sugar
> 3-4 Tbsp Flax Seed (optional)
> 3 eggs
> 1c vegetable oil
> 3oz powdered dry milk
> 1c water

Easy Homemade Christmas Gifts 2014

Directions:
1. Combine wheat flour, bread flour, wheat germ, salt, and brown sugar, and flax seed in mixing bowl. Stir in eggs and vegetable oil.
2. Dissolve dry milk in water, then incorporate the mixture.
3. Mix to form a very firm dough that is smooth and workable.
4. Adjust by adding a little extra flour or water as required.
5. Cover the dough and set aside to relax for 15-20 min.
6. Roll the dough out to 1/2" (1.2cm) thick. Cut out biscuits using a bone-shaped cutter 3"x1.5" (7.5×3.7cm). Place the biscuits on sheet pans lined with baking paper.
7. Bake at 375°F (190°C) for approx. 40 minutes or until biscuits are brown and, more importantly, rock-hard. Let biscuits cool, then store in a covered container. Use as needed to reward your four-legged friends.

EASY TWO-INGREDIENT HOMEMADE DOG TREATS

Ingredients:
2 cups 100% organic whole wheat flour
2 jars of pureed baby food

Directions:
1. Preheat oven to 350°.
2. Mix ingredients together to form a stiff dough. If necessary, add extra flour or water as needed.
3. On a lightly floured surface, roll dough out evenly until it's about 1/4 inch thick. Use cookie cutters to cut into desired shape or a pizza cutter to make cubes.
4. Line a cookie sheet with parchment paper, place treats about 1/2 inch apart. Bake for 20 – 25 minutes.
5. Allow to cool completely before storing in a paper bag.

And that's it!, this recipe makes a lot and lasts for a few weeks.

Katie Cotton
HOMEMADE DOG TREATS RECIPE

Ingredients

2 cups +1/2 half cup rolled oats

½ teaspoon salt

1 egg

½ cup unsalted, low-fat beef broth or chicken broth

Instructions

1. Preheat oven to 325 degrees.

2. Add 2 cups oats, salt, beef broth, and egg to a large mixing bowl. Combine well. Add remaining ½ cup of rolled oat and combine.

3. Pour onto wax paper and knead dough for about 3 minutes. Let stand for about 3 minutes to begin to become firmer. Press to ½-inch thickness.

4. Cut with cutter and place onto a parchment paper lined baking sheet.

5 Bake for 20 minutes. Remove from oven and allow to cool completely.

6. Store in an airtight container for use or store in a zip top bag in the freezer for later thawing and use.

PAW-PRINT DOG TREATS

Ingredients
.
2 cups all-purpose flour, plus more for surface

1/2 cup wheat germ

1/2 cup brewer's yeast

2 teaspoons salt

3 tablespoons canola oil

1 1/2 cups homemade or store-bought low-sodium chicken stock

1. Preheat oven to 400 degrees. Line 2 baking sheets with parchment. Combine flour, wheat germ, brewer's yeast,

and salt in a large bowl. Place canola oil in a large bowl. Add flour mixture to oil in 3 additions, alternating with 1 cup stock; mix until combined.

2. Knead the dough on a lightly floured surface for 2 minutes (dough will be sticky). Roll out dough into 1/4-inch thickness. Cut out rounds using a 2-inch fluted cutter.

4. Transfer to baking sheets. Make an indentation toward the bottom of 1 circle using your thumb, then press dough to make an arch of 4 small circles on top of the thumb print using the tip of your pinky. Repeat with remaining rounds.

5. Freeze for 15 minutes. Bake for 20 minutes, rotating sheets and lightly brushing with remaining 1/2 cup chicken stock halfway through. Turn oven off, and let stand in oven for 40 minutes. Store in an airtight container for use or store in a zip top bag in the freezer for later use.

ABOUT THE AUTHOR

Katie Cotton comes from a big family, with three older brothers, and a dad who worked away a lot. Katie learned how her mom managed to keep a family of five on a budget and still have so many fun times as a family. As Katie got older, and had a family herself, she remembered what her mom had taught her, and now, she too, is a stay at home mom, with two sons of her own, and a husband in the armed forces.

In her series of books on cooking, and gift giving, she shares the wealth of knowledge she has gained through research and experimentation. Katie delights in showing her readers how to stay on a budget and that, with a little preparation- meal times can be quick, cheap and healthy. As well her gift and decorating ideas are delightful, even elegant-and always fun to make plus really help to keep the home budget healthy too. Follow her on Twitter # katiecotton99

EXCERPT SECTION

Best Christmas Cookie Recipes: Easy Holiday Cookies 2014

Are you looking for a way to make this Christmas extra special? Are you tired of all the commercialism and the crazy spending? Then why not try adding a personal touch to your gift baskets by making these super-cute Christmas cookies! Anybody, young or old, will love these thoughtful gifts, and you're guaranteed to bring a smile to their faces, and make their day!

EXCERPT: Soft Gingerbread Cookies

Ingredients:

1 ½ cup dark molasses
1 cup packed brown sugar
2/3 cups cold water
1/3 cup shortening

Katie Cotton

7 cups all-purpose flour
2 teaspoons baking soda
1 teaspoon salt
1 teaspoon ground allspice
2 teaspoon ground ginger
1 teaspoon ground cinnamon
1 teaspoon ground cloves

Instructions:

1. Mix molasses, brown sugar, water and shortening.
2. Mix in remaining ingredients.
3. Cover and refrigerate at least 2 hours.
4. Heat oven to 350 degrees F.
5. Roll dough ¼ inch thick on floured board.
6. Cut with floured gingerbread cutter or other favorite shaped cutter.
7. Place about 2 inches apart on a lightly greased cookie sheet.
8. Bake until no indentation remains when touched, 10 to 12 minutes; cool.
9. Decorate with frosting, if desired.

Easy Homemade Christmas Gifts 2014

Easy and Fun Homemade Christmas Ornaments and Decorations

Do you want to give an unusual and personal gift? If so, then the "Easy and Fun Homemade Ornaments" book is for you! Packed full of great ideas for homemade Christmas decorations, for your tree and around your home, these decorations will brighten up any tree, or any room.

EXCERPT: Jingle Bell Candle Jar

What You'll Need
Wide-mouth mason jar
Votive candle
Filler (Epsom salt, pebbles, sand, etc.)
Jute twine
Jingle bells
Spray glitter

1. Fill a mason jar with Epsom salt or other filler and nestle a votive candle into it. Wrap the mouth of the jar with jute twine strung with a few jingle bells. If you like more precision, glue the

twine down in perfect rows. Otherwise, go for a more casual random look.

2. If you want to be more creative, paste some paper snowflakes on the twine and spray with glitter.

www.ingramcontent.com/pod-product-compliance
Ingram Content Group UK Ltd.
Pitfield, Milton Keynes, MK11 3LW, UK
UKHW022120230426
12048UKWH00010BA/629